So dynamic, supple, and keenly attentive to the natural world, Jory Mickelson's *All This Divide* allows the reader to contemplate our teeming days, our shared treasure house of planetary paradoxes: time coupled with alluring Nature as mighty destroyers and clarifiers ("what if the lake / was a century instead?"); propulsive history as instilling primer and stubborn obstacle. In this memorable, compelling book Mickelson meditates on the annals and inspiriting beauty of The American West and Southwest, the demesne as a vital realm of open spaces, heave-ho greed, and artful dreaming—all the while sustaining a poetry of adept music and rousing imagery, of daily reverence, sweeping empathy, and clear-eyed investigation.
    —Cyrus Cassells, 2021 Texas Poet Laureate

"The hard line of horizon draws the eye, always forward," writes Jory Mickelson as they guide us in this richly-drawn pastoral of the American West. Like Whitman, Mickelson celebrates the natural world in great detail both in its landscapes and in the people who inhabit them. *All This Divide* is a beautiful and sensual collection that takes as it purpose "…to make every image true, or at least true enough to last."
    —C. Dale Young, author of *Prometeo*

Jory Mickelson's *All This Divide* circumambulates through time, excavating the violent layers of lineage: "Our story / one dark furrow." Mickelson's images are sharp and evocative, imaginative and felt: "The swallows— // they are combing the clouds' trailing hair" and "the knotted // hawk you are / pulling from my throat." Lyrical and sonically curious, these poems press their ears against the hearts of many storytellers. *All This Divide* asks us to consider our connectedness, one beetle and one stone at a time.
    —Jane Wong, author of *Meet Me Tonight in Atlantic City*

Jory Mickelson deftly and powerfully probes one of the great American myths through breathtaking poem after breathtaking poem. Mickelson's daring reckoning with the idea of The West (its plundered opening, its brutal hunger and astonishing beauty) is balanced by their deep empathy and eye for complexity, pleasure, and detail. "The history of loss / sets up a people to either forget / or hold on forever," Mickelson writes, and these poems are both prayer and commentary on the horror and holiness of that history and its modern echoes. This is a necessary work of unsorrowing and unforgetting that is utterly gorgeous to read, alive with music, buoyed by skillful research and rendering, and ultimately brimming with mercy, hope, and light. I am awed by these poems.

 —Corrie Williamson,
  author *The River Where You Forgot My Name* and *Sweet Husk*

All This Divide **is both a reckoning**—with the myths and violences of westward expansion, with the beautiful and ravaged landscapes of the American West, with the soul and soul›s ache for holiness—as well as an intimate, lyrical exploration of what remains of Stegner's geography of hope, which includes, in Mickelson's queer retelling, the hungering heart and the body of the beloved. I haven't read a book as simultaneously fierce and lovely in a long, long time.

 —Joe Wilkins,
  author of *Fall Back Down When I Die* and *When We Were Birds*

All This Divide

Jory Mickelson

Spuyten Duyvil

New York City

Library of Congress Control Number: 2024937124

We are instructed by those objects that come to speak to us…
—Mark Doty

What is it then between us?
What is the count of the scores or hundreds of years between us?
—Walt Whitman

CONTENTS

Sometimes the truth

Sometimes the truth

depends on a walk
around the lake,
the philosopher said.
What if the lake
is a century instead?
If time upends all
principals, tips them
into graves—then
it's up to the actors,
placed on a makeshift
stage. What stories

do they voice? Hollow
tubes run between history's
walls, where we press
our ears to catch some
faint sighing. *We*
always knew
hunger…
we knew where the owl
spent his days…
there was
blood
on the grass, nothing
else to be found.

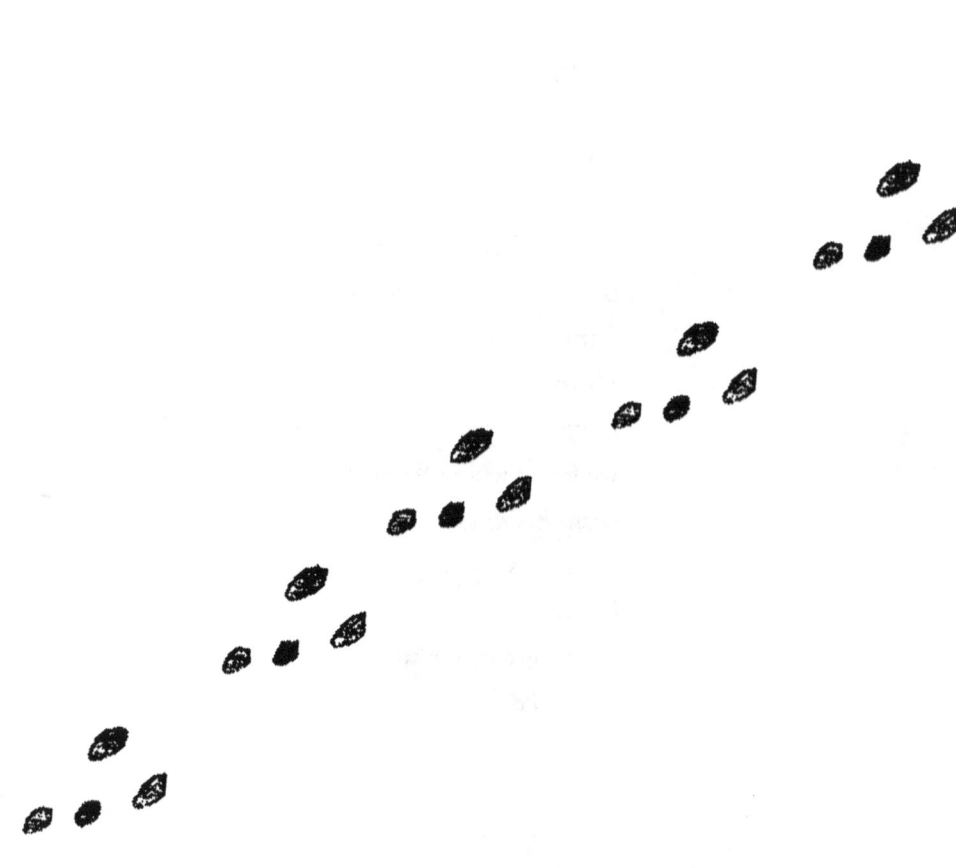

SECTION 1

IN APRIL

Who has time for a diamond?
I want a field, where birds

genuflect as they peck for food.
At the edges, sword ferns

rattle their blades in recognition.
All grasses wear the rain

as lace. The hawthorn's a new
green heraldry of bud. The swallows—

they are combing the clouds' trailing hair.

Through the Imagined House's Door, Horizons Come

This country is a kingdom
                    I would make for myself.

Dressed in the susurrous ocean
                    of grass & lap

of wind, without one subject
                    but myself.

I know all I have before me
& all the burden I've

stored up, whole decades
                    to unsorrow. Tomorrow

I'll begin, but today this
                    patch of unspoiled & infinite

wave. Tomorrow
                    then, the sundering,

but today I step into green
opening before me as God

went before Moses—behind me
                    it closes, signaling

no road, no ship,
                    no angel to ferry me

back to the grey

        house of my birth. Today

let me rejoice & smoke a little, forget
I'd ever had this face.

PLUNDER: SHOVEL

Gravely, more gravely
than a blade's shuck,

the digging itself
wakes what is sleeping,

can only wake
with its excavating

of earth, unblankets
the sleeper to noon's

sweet honey some
might call light.

Taste, how pleasing
the moment

of rising after
such dormancy.

WHAT DISTANCE DID I KNOW?

The pacing of the river from
the house, the expansion of my father's reach
year by year, beyond the town, the routing of supplies like water

wending its way from maker to boat to seller's
hands. The extension of the priest's *orans*, the floating lace,
the hang of the chasuble's dull gold. The breadth of the voice unfolding

my imagination from Antwerp to
the New World. Red dirt of Kentucky, the Cherokee,
the crumbled empire of Napoleon, given away, the West. What could be

done at twenty, or in just twenty years?
The journey beginning with an island. Begin with
a stretching of the neck toward horizon, with a vessel, the sea.

FIELD

Here, in the pool
of your moan I rub
      my stubble against our

dumb pleasure. Your laughter
sparks evergreen in the long
      grass, this lazy field, where even,

if you'll excuse my bragging, even
your scuffed jeans have collapsed
      at my skill for bringing you

to the fringe, the very hem
of wind before we are both
      blown open—spread

entirely like this
red blanket your legs
      pin me to. My tongue

tunes insect-hum at your
ear. Songmaker, soon you'll
      make me sing for you. How

you wanted to earlier
in the car, as we drove
      toward this expanse

and quickly it comes—
what I wanted to
            become, the knotted

hawk you are
pulling from my throat.

Into the Wilderness

The stream strewn, loggered-up
with bodies. Thick with bent
limbs & bloat, the blur of bird
wing. Before the harvest, the well-
ordered crops of grey & blue.
Smoke & clamor, the red
fruit—men packed into formation
& graves. Tumult of the South's
green becoming orange
with flame & if a bayonet can
open a man, then what
about the West?

~~

Room to lose himself in,
forget the ordered horror
of war—unspoiled—everything
awaiting his touch (or so
he thinks)—land unrolled like carpet & how
a man can't imagine the pattern
he'd put down until he knows
the bounds of fiber, the ends
of weft. (History is written, but
in this space, it's unimagined yet.)

~~

A cultured & sensitive man
beset by financial problems & later
a grizzly.
But this account has been
lost & unable to be
resurrected on the page
& here, history
is already made
& is in the making, so
let us begin. The war
receding, the wind picking
up & St. Louis no longer
outpost, but not yet center
of a nation, an ever-hungry realm.

THE FLYER CALLED IT A SPACIOUSNESS
Homestead Flyer

Garden of the World—Free
Lands to the West,
it's nothing but a vacancy,
all that ethereal sky.
       Great Original blank spot
of plains, of range, unwavering sun.
Days of expressionless dust
& rock & furnace of wind
putting emptiness on display.
       What to make of such
silence in which night birds, insects,
dimhunters rowl & roil
in the caliginous grass. There is
no refreshment found in sleep.
       Some Almighty Hand
plucked every tree from soil
so not even shade at evening
prevails to give us rest.
       For the turning
of the wooden wheel, endless
creak & chime of tack, oxen
straining in their yoke. The rounding
burn of days, our sweat,
an eternal track.
       There is only one story
& it goes on repeating
in the waste, that no god
could make this landscape hospitable.

It tells us
if we were the salt
of the earth, we've been cast
into the ruts
to be trodden on.

TRIANGULATION

Snow crenellates what is
sleeping: sod buck
house, bare-hooved horse
who's thrown her last shoe.

How fire needs
several views to be
located, to be, finally
extinguished.

Parallax of human
bodies drawn down
the generations. Our story
one dark furrow.

Plunder: Gold before its Discovery

Leave me to my grave. I prefer
the grum, the graveled dark.

There is drinking to be done, wagers
to lose around a fire. Leave off

the shovel. Leave the pickaxe to its
dull glint. Ready for sleep. Don't dream

of me, my laden body. Forget this course
entirely. You'll make a better life back home.

.

Welcome to the Hi-Line

The land and the wheat that never cared who touched it, or why.
Larry Levis

There, almost smudged, a mountain named
after some relative, branched just
past the family tree, gone pale

like pages loosening from a ledger. The hard
line of horizon draws the eye, always
forward, every direction beveled

by lens of sky. No matter how far a person
travels, they'll remain centered, compass-
poised—field after field.

Take Thomas, who at fourteen, was unable
to sit still on the train funneling
west, outrunning his stepfather,

weighted down with a small
inheritance the stepfather said he'd kill
the boy to get. The train pushed

Thomas deeper into prairie, into a life
breaking sod. It would take three generations
to build up the farm: locust, hail, drought,

tent worm, June snow, blight, tornado, wind.
Not even the caragana (the only vertical)
that hugs the road rindled in countless

rows will do anything but fail
against the wind, which never ceases
changing its mind about coming and going.

Trace Highway 2 on any map, the land's
paper flat. Going east you'll stretch a line
through Chester, Joplin, Rudyard, Hingham

and Kremlin to Chinook, where the Milk
River churns or dwindles, but is never
the color of its name. The town in February

aims to receive any warm wind to thaw
its rigid face, a compass rose, petaled
for months in white. The wind pushes

everything, will bank snow two stories
high against a house. Even generations can
be set to drift, blown to other ground

the way Thomas' granddaughter (from a distance)
divines her profits, the price of wheat each year
against the taxes on the land. Finally, she

sells to the neighbor who's been leasing
it for years; the farm undone, small denomination
lifted from hand and set to air.

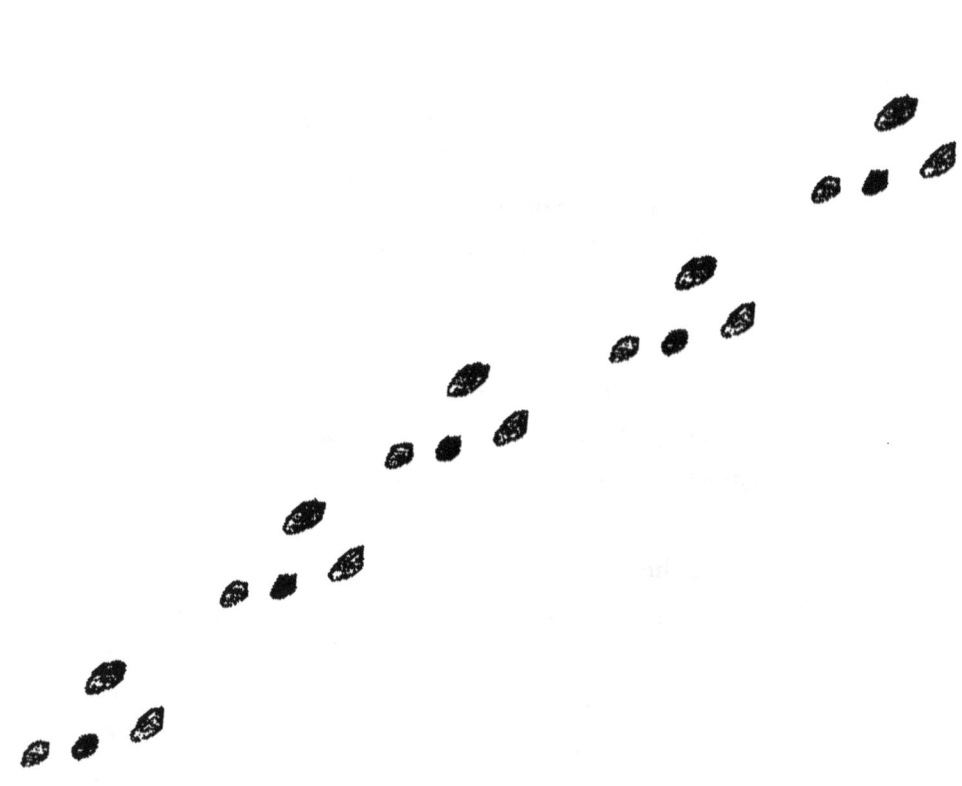

SECTION 2

BEAUTIFUL COUNTRY

Oh beautiful, Oh country,
I didn't want to love all your green,
but I let myself. How beauty
folds in on the heart before
you even begin to know
it. I thought, yes I would
kill the one who tried to
take this place from me, if
it were mine. How I never
thought I could commit to
beauty with such violence—
and how, given our violent histories,
no naming can save us.
Two-Heart Butte—so much wonder
a single heart couldn't hold
it, but named in truth for two
Blackfoot men Meriwether Lewis
murdered. How the history of loss
sets up a people to either forget
or hold on forever. How beauty
dares us to change our minds.
Perhaps the earth can allow
what's been placed deep
to be, not buried, but maybe
called to rest instead. And how
what is resting can fold in on itself
as it begins to dream of embracing
you and everyone who meets
at this rise. I would call this
shrinking space between us home.

ON JOSH KILPATRICK WHO DROWNED
after Bruce Snider

All day the river gives its common blessing:
yellow stonefly, quartz, a fisherman's
filament tangled in snag. A sandpiper
runs the muddy bank. Resting here,
pink child's shirt, sleeve torn. Here

rests: driftwood, thistle, dogshit.
All day God makes old souls into new
just past the Conoco station, the pulp
mill & Bunker Ammo on Hwy 93.
Quaking aspens shake themselves
free, yellow coins to spend in creeks

& strip mall parking lots. Seventh Day
Adventists miss the farmers' market
where Hutterites sell fresh bread and onions
cheap. Shortly frost will cover it all, even
the junk Camaro in the gravel lot. Even

the mountain ash, whose berries get
the sparrows drunk. Forgotten, the river says,
means too late. Whatever it was you came for—
gone. The season goes, leaves the doe
to browse the last stand of alfalfa curing
in the field about to be mown, baled away.

A River Is
after Deborah Digges

A river is
a prayer
    of its own
        making. I don't
know what water

    prays to. Amid those
mumbled sentiments we
        resisted and surrendered
        our bodies
        as Naaman did before

    to the idea of the ordinary,
but we
        relished in our
        everyday
        forms, the common wet,

    the unremarkable
sun who rose
mute and unblemished
        each August
        morning. My mother,

    I watched her at this
distance, she never
        appeared more beautiful
        than with her
        arms outstretched, almost

dancing, her whole self
worshiping
       the current. Oh River,
      let me
     always remember

  the trivial, what goes
unmarked, and if
       remembering can be
     a prayer,
    in this smallness

  let me
grow broad:
a river at flood.

PLUNDER: THE COMPANY

Under every green tree
a burning of measurement

in cord & board foot, in tons
of ore: gold, silver, lead.

Seven pounds of meat
per day, five pounds of flour

per week, the contract said.
Timber needed to build

the works, to build the mines,
to build the town, the tracks

running out. The smelter eats
seven hundred cords of wood per day,

devours all the ore someone
can bring & more, refines nature's

handiwork with heat & cyanide,
releases what shines within.

IN TIME THE SNOW IS GONE

sometimes the maple, sometimes
the water birches

a field of green
harebell and tulips too

the brown hare turning
away from the radish greens

something like the dark
left beneath the bank of spruce

the morning light coming
through the window

mixed with rain

she said the kitchen is clean
but could use a sprucing

needle-scent, sap, newly
painted trim

the shape of planks
outlined, newspaper laid

to catch paint
something pink obscuring

the text, in time
the snow is gone and the grass

To the River

Oh, take me to the river to wash
these clothes stiff with sweat

from the grime of daily   toil, take me to the water
to scour dishes with river

sand. Take me to the river   bank to gather dripping bucketfuls
for our thirst,

to wet flour into bread,   to boil every scrap & speck
into soup. Take me slowly

into the current's pool   to bathe the burnt & chafing
skin of this tired body.

Take me to the river   to gather heavy mud for plaster, thick
clay to make a crooked pot, gather

a hundred kinds of green   to feed, to heal
to cut willows,

bend them to every kind   of use. Oh, take me to collect
eggs from nests, capture

fish, mollusks, water   creatures, known and unknown.
Take me to the river's heavy

cool, its thousand flies &   mosquitos. As we have taken,
as we have gladly received,

may this tributary, this
bluechange course go on.

PLUNDER: REVOLVER

Your right hand has grasped for
me; now the gate may not

be shut. I loosen the mouth
and quicken the heart in

its shadowed chest. Equip you
to break the best and worst;

to me, there is no difference.
I make well-being & create

calamity. I do not cause
this darkness, but draw it forth

from within you, spring the lock
of desire or dread. My six hot

stars are a constellation called
surety. I am the lord of this

place, an idol weeping tears
of lead, the spoiled fruit

of all your reaching.

SECTION 3

Friday Night, Bannack

Because the cowboy asks me to, I rise
in the smoke-filled room. We greet
shyly as at the start of courtship, hats tipped
back on our heads—moons behind a cloud
of hair, then we step hard through the fiddle's
unremitting saw, the pressbox's exhalation,
a song that raises our feet despite the long
hours in the saddle or the mine, work
that's given us our rough hands. But these hands
can't offer relief with such delicate maneuvers.
The failure of women to appear—the ones
we left at home across the country, who love us
or will someday. We will build toward that
hour of square wooden buildings, window glass, lace,
where a woman is fit to be seen.

                                    We increase
our speed as the tempo builds and the rollicking
of our bodies pressed like slices of roughneck bread
sandwiching the tune between us. Our
sweat sluicing us in salt, in musk, in cheap
liquor coming out our pores. The man who asks
is the man who leads over the rise
of the melody's swelling. Each step
stamps our desire into the gapped boards
of the floor. We shed nearly all at the spin—
the work and what this way of living's made us.

I AM AWARE

of how careful
these last days
of summer are,

but remain uncertain

whether I
am driven
or being drawn.

I thought

I heard an unknown
bird calling me.

What makes a place

holy? Can a song?
What then,
when the last note

leaves?

WE SAY THE DRIFTER LEFT IN THE NIGHT

In the rough-cut church, serious women
plow the day with their prayers,
spade hard their narrow way

toward God. To know what they loved,
they left it. Only in absence
could they tell its true shape.

They write: *the grass is lush, the soil black*
as sin. The deer and the cattle fatten
themselves without effort.

I thirst, says the man
hanging from the tree as the roots
store up any gladness which falls from him.

How a cloud on the horizon—
it blurs as it reforms. At its height,
the heat causes deer to long,

as the convicted might, for water, a cool
place to lie. Perhaps in the shade—
which the tree gathers with such

abundance. Rest. You are weary,
tired enough to ignore the flutter
of his cotton shirt in the breeze.

Plunder: religion

Shall the axe boast
over the grip of the executioner?

The basket glory in its weave,
its ability to catch, against

the weaver? If so, what
of the stained wood block, the cross

smirching dully, cleaving the clean
black of the minister's chest? True

righteousness is a tool made well,
completes its purpose. Let nothing

boast above the hand which
has fashioned it.

GOD'S JUDGMENT

What if we've gotten the judgment
of God wrong all this time? Light
implacable, yes, that works its way

surely across the narrow valley
illuminating every last blade
of grass, every corner in the closet

of every house finally and rightly—
all that sure gold light. Yet, it doesn't
burn, no spotlight or interrogator's

lamp, nor focusing lens held up
to sizzle, no, but something
more like the easy

light of a barn and God's judgment
less cruel than we'd imagined.
Something more

like each of us showing
our beloved cantankerous
heifer at the fair, whom we have

so carefully washed and trimmed,
bedded in sweet straw—not set for
condemnation at last. But to show

off & display our hard effort, even if
we, prideful, stand before the judge
saying look how many hours

I've given to this sweet-faced, sway-
hipped Guernsey before you. Doesn't
her coat gleam, the liquid eyes,

the transparent and lovely stretch
of her ear? It's in this light God,
humbler than we'd guessed,

kinder too—with both
seriousness and a smile
—runs his old hand along

the haunch of our beasts,
takes pleasure in the clean shape,
and all the evil and hard words

we'd feared were only our own
voice in the dark stall of our
hearts, fed and watered with their

heavy bucket of doubts.
All the while, God's judgment
of our work is done with gentleness,

pointing out the best parts saying,
"My, fine animal you've brought.
I bet this one took all your effort,

I know, I've been there myself."
God telling us all the while
what a good job we've done

even if there are one or two others
ahead of us in line.

LONGHAIR

*General George Custer napping somewhere
along the Yellowstone River, 1873*

My hair is long and fine
      and I am known for it.
I keep it well-groomed as Sampson,
      his unshorn locks the secret
to his strength. I imagine
      the Lord too had hair
as long as mine or longer, fine
      as mine or finer to behold;
he was the Lord after all.
      God's pure ornament or instrument,
depending on where you are
      reading. I too, am an adornment
or instrument given my purpose
      at the moment. I too,
of my own vanity am aware, when taking
      my violence into the field.
Many a thing is made of pride
      uncountable, but I take
mine in the terror
      I am able to loose; few are
able to match my vengeance.
      I do not fabricate.
But this afternoon, for an hour,
      let no god be
god, only the earth
      or the hour itself, here
in this low valley. O, Mountain.
      O, Sky. I will call you glorious

and I a flower in your field
      not working this hour, not spinning
but spindling light, weaving
      my rest like a flag
as I recline. Let the dirt
      beneath me hold all
I need for today. White
      as the lily of the field,
my skin, where underclothes reveal it.
      I surrender to the light.
Easeful, I will not turn away,
      but attend it, so we might
not be lost.

SISTER SELF
after Michael Garrigan

Sometimes I think
we went there
in a dream

(together still) lodged
inside the sleeping
body of the boy

I used to be.

WINTER'S GAME

In an empty field I dream
of bread. Hunger's not an axiom

for longing when the dim oven
of the stomach's lain cool for weeks.

Sugar, salt, potatoes—gone—flour
nothing but memory. Each roll

I've eaten, I remember it
by heart and in vain. Winter's game:

see if she can last just shy
of eternity. In the cold, I go to sleep

dreaming of Christ in the mountains
turning stones into golden loaves,

dream my fields full of heavy-headed grain.
The bitter rooms of winter fill themselves

with endless, wanting light. Come spring,
what's left of me will leaven only grass.

WYETH: HEAVEN

The afterlife was spare: iron-framed
bed, homespun sheets. Bedside,

a hollow pressboard box with tender
red interior. The stern window

said, *empty valley full
of grass*, and this is

where I wondered at
how I'd come to be

alone with such silence,
no one had yet to

pierce. Light
sifted itself between

the peaks to fall
on the scuffless grass. The wind

riffling & quietful until there
was nothing to the world

but the soft rasp of
grass on grasses on grass

If Walt Whitman Can Be in a Berkeley Supermarket, Allen Ginsberg Can Be in Montana in 1851

What thoughts I have of you today, Allen,
sitting in the yard while Siberian Elm leaves shower
yellow, half-blinded looking at all this glimmer & light.

In my endless transposing I put you on the edge
of a bison herd, see you wooly-bearded
with your thousands of exclamation points!!!

The brown shag of their humps and swiveling
small eyes! A few hungry-tongued wolves cruising
& casing at the outward side. Magpies on bison backs!

Allen, I saw you, bespectacled, ecstatic
old self-promoter, in your Indian (not Indigenous) kurta
& beads, digging your bare feet into the dirt,
looking for peyote.

I heard you chant at those buffalo.
Moloch! Holy, holy, HOLY! Buddha death. Dharma death.
Who—Who—Who—

Your smoldering bardic vision, wandering through that
unending herd, calling it samsara, following an
old bull, believing each humped beast a bodhisattva.

Crisscrossing through the scattered ponderosa
sniffing their private vanilla scent, plucking
tri-bundled needles, chewing sweet sap without
cutting down a single tree. To leave
everything intact is unamerican.

The horizon infinite & ruddy. Sun
never quite setting. Allen, where to next? Will we swim
these rivers white men are just beginning to name?
Jefferson, Madison, Gallatin. Will we live the endless day
alone in some unpopulated dream, or be welcomed

or warred upon by the people, who for countless
generations, are already home?

At Three Forks,
water adds to water so it can race toward that Zen
Mississippi koan.

The Famous Western Artist Gives a Lecture

In the artist's studio, notice
        how the form occupies

a space—then to dress it. Open
        the wooden boxes, rummage
        through the shelves—here

the moccasins I love,
        have painted eleven times,
        notice the beaded

green. They are Kiowa or Lakota,
        I don't remember.

With the proper costume,
        nearly any muscled form
        will fill my need. In my time,

I've turned white men into
        Indians, though to do it I made
        my neighbor shave his beard.

I'm in the business
        of making art, painting

to bring back the West
        for those who only
        imagine its expanse.

I document these tribes before
                they disappear—

turn them into art before they're
                nothing more than artifact.
                The artist must cede

some history might be
                beyond his skill. But I believe,
                the nature of a thing

is truly seen only once
                I put it down, an immemorial

view. Without exception,
                it is the artist's job to make
                each rendering exceptional, exact.

So, it hardly matters if a Crow
                wears a Chippewa robe or the tipi's

pattern is borrowed
                from a dream—that's artistic
                license, what makes one's genius known.

My role to make every image true,
                or at least true enough to last.

Tilework Illustration of Fox Among Grapevines

The yolk's lush
on the fox's dark tongue—

mosaic of shell in the dirt

—all the generations come
down to this bright furrow.

They built us a nest,

no promise of security
only a hope for it.

We were only ever invisible

when our mothers hovered
over us, but now, these

new-pitched bodies make

their own demands.
Even as the light quietly fills

the foliage, as the fruit

begins to soften. We knew
what was left to us, as something

low in the field quietly approaches.

[WHEN GOD WASN'T GOD]

When god wasn't god
he was

an animal like us,
but less

skin. Not less than
we, but

more leather and light,
his smile

a curved claw used
to open

new possibility, the tufts
of fur

crowning pointed ears
primal grace.

How then did we pray?
for mercy

never to see holiness
coming

for us among the trees.

Slowly Now the Shadows Lengthen

Soon the deer will come
to the pond. The pinks
of their tongues cooled
by water—they strengthen me—

I would call this desiring home

Let your figure tarry
with me, ghostshape
in my remembering. I am lonely
without your silhouette quickening

the night star. You are with me

when I close my eyes. Rest
your head against me
like a teal hen set
in the sleep of her nest.

Upward and trackless they go

my words parting nothing,
not distance, not longing.
Prayers scatter like chaff,
the fade of ember rising.

This isn't paradise

though it would be easy
to believe in if you were
beside me. A kingdom
is just an emptiness

unless there is another

with whom to divide it—
heavy, bitter-skinned
wild summer plum
honeyed to its stone.

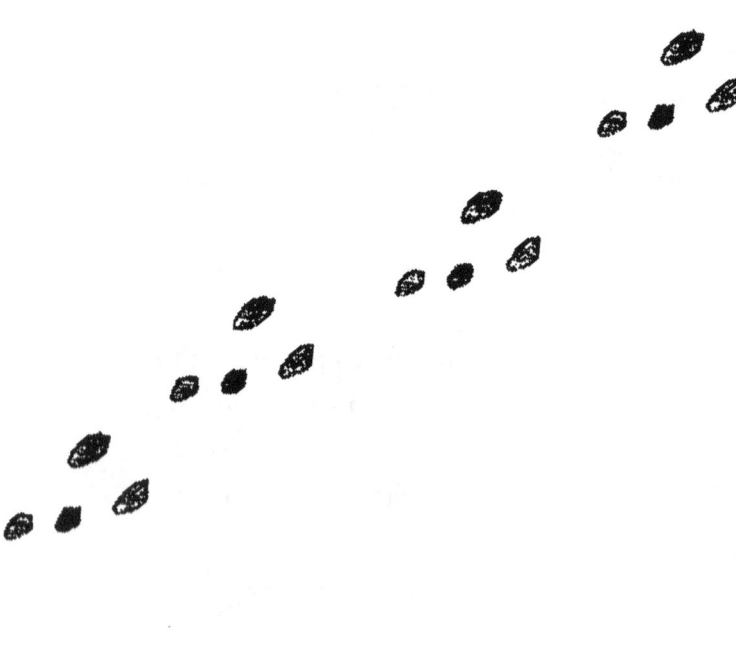

SECTION 4

CONVERGENCE// //CONVERSION

A Power, a Power has
shown Shining Shirt
a vision, told him
there was Good
& Evil that the People
knew little about.
But men would come
with pale skin
& long black skirts.
Men would come
to teach the People
a new medicine,
teach them Good
from Evil & give
the People new
names & new laws
to govern them.
The unknown god
was called Amotkan
he-who-lives-
on-high. When
these pale men
come in their
long black skirts,
soon all wars
will cease but
it will also mean
the end of the People
living on this land

At the first Salish delegation to
St. Louis, Governor Clark had long
since forgotten the language, so
they waited the winter for someone
to come who might translate.
Black Eagle & Speaking Eagle
died, were buried. Come spring
No Horns On His Head died of
illness & Rabbit Skin Leggings
was killed by Blackfeet returning
home. On the second journey, Insula
only met Protestants & returned.
The third delegation—Big Ignace
& his sons—he left them in
St. Louis with money to be
educated, but their mother missed
them so much, she journeyed by
herself to bring them back. Eighteen
months later, Big Ignace went again,
but was killed by the Sioux. Finally
Young Ignace & Little Ignace,
the sons of Big Ignace, brought
a letter to the Bishop of St. Louis
written for them by an Iroquois.
This, the fourth delegation,
the successful one, where they
meet the Jesuit Pierre-Jean
De Smet, who travels with them
in the spring the following year, joins

forever. The People the Salish in the Bitterroot,
will become slaves, & Shining Shirt's prophecy
this is how it will be—begins to be fulfilled.

Watchman You Become the Hour

Dark summer moon. White moths
clothing the heavens like sackcloth
set with lights. The restless traveler borne
away by their need. Along the road, the estuary
salts itself to barrenness. Tree roots
choke on the whiteness of fish bone and rot.
Summer evaporating the sea, leaving

a winter scene, everything rimed in frost.
We didn't perceive its accumulation.
We were able to ignore the whirl-
wind, the tempest. But no more. Too late
for the windless grass, the untilled field,
the house's soured well. Yesterday's heat
kindles itself into morning. Already
we feel its seep. Look to the stone,
the light says. Soon you will be set back
into the quarry from which you were hewn.

PLUNDER: RESIDENTIAL SCHOOL

The children are, at last, asleep.
Like bright brass plates we've stamped them

with new names: Peter, Rachel, Levi,
Esther, Aaron, Ruth. Each day's lesson

is how to forget a bend of river,
word for willow, your grandmother's hands.

We cut your hair. Release it
easily as smoke. I promise sadness doesn't last

if you let it go. Learn this new word
heaven, a better life that awaits you,

it is this one.

CORRESPONDENCE

Your letter has come.

Someone's died. Someone has

divorced. I want to

eat your grief like bread.

It was snowing out the window—

the lilacs all lay down

veiled like too-young brides.

Why do I keep this

cup that's cracked, the saucer

missing? I have put off

opening your letter. Soon

this cup, the snow, will break.

CORRECTNESS

I have often mistaken
            the movement of leaves
for the leaves themselves.
            Knowing what the water did
yesterday I take no notice
            of the lake's variance,
the rippled difference
            in the hour I pass.
Writing ten poems about walking
            around bodies of water,
I ignore what each landscape is
            doing on its own.
So, another loop around this track
            of thought, as the cottonwoods
continue their early shimmer.
            When I saw what he wrote,
heard what she said, learned
            what they thought—
I became certain of them, their mistakes,
            wanted to correct each
error, fix their rustling leaves
            to their crooked branches
with my sharp, decisive pins. Neaten
            the lake's folds
into what I find acceptable.
            Attention is not always the start
of devotion, when judgment pulls
            at the lead, eager dog

to be on its way. This morning, let me
                too be changeable, uncertain.
Shake me,
                until I lose myself
in all that cordate movement, one
among so much dancing green.

Reading the Book of Isaiah as Wildfires Burn

It is summer and my church
is made of birds,

winged god
in lenticular view, as if to define

the shape could set
a form, a boundary to

the fathomless, a name

made of syllables lifted
to blue rudiment.

The seraphs were proto-
types for six-legged flyers:

sweat bee, salmon fly, hooktip moth,
caught in the hem, a hymn

of his robe, wind greening through leaves.

Then a raiment: "to array,"
to be adorned with rain.

We adore water amid drought,
how dryness precipitates

a leaner devotion:
the narrow path amid dust

or needle duff and still

from May to August the bark
beetle works its faith

cloistered to the inner gallery
of fir, until it too

has earned its glorious
crown. We want

the holy heat without

the flame. Isaiah warned
that at the sound

of the angels' voices, the thresholds
shook, the temple filled

with smoke—that no winged thing
can save. That the lengthening

of days may also be the end.

Beginning with a Line by Mildred Walker

and you've gone on all these years
hating each other, opinions frozen hard

like late March ground, the air raw.
Unremittent sky by day, dark and sulky.

By night the stark handle-stars,
celestial oxen, furrow black heaven—

still your heart is a broken door,
useless, askew in a week of wind.

Even in stillness you hear
hate roar between your ears, summer and winter

resentment buckles you,
warps you beyond all ken. You're good

for nothing now, but burning. Light a fire,
heave each spite from its pile, drag it

down into the cinders. It flares red,
lighting your rough-dug grave or hers.

Another Bird at the End of an Elegy

I am not far
       from my own
       dying. This body's house

harvests whole families
       of grief. Who can pray?
       All I want to do

is sleep. To quit this
       intolerable living, the endless
       & ever scrolling light

of the city's glassy weight.
       I have nothing
       against my life,

its good hours, when I hold
       myself to myself
       for no other

reason than to declare myself
       ordinary, as a crabapple
       in bloom. It blazes,

not caring no one will
       eat its fruit.
       This morning light

reckons a judgment,
     oppresses, rather than
     consoles. Let the clouds

come. Let the wind-stripped tree
     in the yard be undone.
     Loneliness—something like

the hoofchurned dirt, a racing
     barrel left
     in the arena. Last night

the stars were a field of grain
     I fed myself
     from; today

the rain is sharper. I am the heavy
river. I am spring's
thin drizzle. I was

not forgiven. Then I remember
     in the sparrow's broken flight
     there is nothing to forgive.

DRAMATURGY

"Now the works of the flesh are obvious…"
—Galatians 5:19

    Misdirection,
spotlit, narrator saying, *Look here, these men*
embraced,
      the shame
of it. As if sin were a banked dark in flood-lit
chiaroscuro.
      As if light
were revelation, as if gesture or illumination were
truth, as though
      narrator
was the voice of god, the voice bestowed by one
proclaiming to
      a passive audience
comfortable in their seats. Consumed and consuming, unable
to know what is
      at work
before the tableau's next reveal: ruined landscape,
graveyard,
      cataclysm.
What does it profit
a man
    to be with
a man, embracing, tender-hearted
and yes,
      naked
if that matters, making love or
just after
      having made it.
Context always

the fuzzy

       part, wobbled

focus when it comes to profit. What

does it

       matter,

these men, their lives against backdrop

of sprawling empire?

PLUNDER: VIGILANTISM

The town was busy as a hive—
a pouring out of angry hooves.

The miner with his pan, with his sluice,
is thieved from under the cover of dark,

through the price of goods. *Malum Non Vide*—
see no evil. To be vigilant

against violence, one must be committed
to violent acts. When the law fails to serve,

let notice be given: we shall live
to see them buried beside the others.

We are calling for decent & orderly
lynching. Bring me my horse,

black & glistening, my rope. If there is
such a place as hell, then this

must be its back door.

THERE IS A DOOR

let's call the door
the sun & when I lie down
like grass at midday I know
only light. As an unrestfullness

on still water only knows
how to extend, so too did
whatever was within
finger its way to the end of the blades

of grass & step into
the air. As a thistle might
or down or the crude paper
lamp & candle we are calling—

a soul? I was laid down
on the earth & the light
shone through me as if
I was nothing more

than empty frame, clear
pane of nothing. The grass
beneath my body, the sun

& this is insufficient & also
all I know, how incomplete
the body of language.

SECTION 5

SXWEXWETCHELI // HUMMINGBIRD

Does our language hold
a word for such green
hovering, as if time
had stopped the rain
to hang a single drop
in air? Do other languages
have a word for this?
Does this green have
a story? I know enough
to know each word
has its own way
of speaking. Why
do I feel entitled to
know it? Why do I
assume you would
give it away?

Cape Disappointment

The meadow moves easy in wind, as a creek
eases its course after flood. The red-tailed hawk
you knew returns, ageless, year after year

to its jumbled pitch of sticks. Fifty years back,

you found your cousin drowned in Tenmile Creek,
there was no saving either of you. Call that
first room home, which turns from

the sight of water. Water can mean

forgiveness or submerge you in your guilt.
I was born in a room, not looking at a meadow,
but the sea. I can only recall its rumbles

& retreats, in these poems that knock

on the front door & run away. I've forgotten
the names of all the people I used to call
my friends. I want the water to

absolve me, rather than remind. I want

a view of the sea that is nothing but grass.
Leave the gulls for the hawk to feed on. If
I could go back—instead light rides the waves

until it fractures & foams. We call this *best*

forget about it & move on. There—
where we can't remember—the stream
continues into the willow, into the night.

Spring, Bitterroot Valley 1848

I love their indelicate folds—
wool among last year's brown
bull thistle, the field's
unshorn crown. Ragged,

sheep dragged in February's
trudge. Yet emerging for Leap Day's arc—

lambs all scatter and kick,
part the coarse grass as a child
splits the curtains to catch
sight of their audience. Mud

in abundance spatters every
coat. These low and lively clouds

fill the world with their blunder,
their mothers, ruminate, count the hours,
kids mumbling the pink
rosary of their teats.

ANTHEM

hoarfrost / splendor
of the grass / o
radiant king

thrush's throat / estuary
and bay / eloquent
dusk song

sea glass / cormorant's bending
neck / your hand cupped
to gather water

field at the end
of spring / nest
of winds / archipelago

horse's left haunch / rough
sawn lumber / the sleep
of an ant's wing

deer mouse / thimbleful
of seed / worn
antler's velvet

false mallow / rumble-bellied
toad / three willows
along the banks

Turkeys in Snow
after Edward Hirsch's "Wild Gratitude"

   Some mornings
when I wake, after sleep
   has wounded me

into wildness, I smile
   saying, "Let's not
talk about any of it

   or climate change or
non-native species and just...
   turkeys in snow..."

The morning so quiet I could
   hear their quirtle and chirr
while they scratched, their ridiculous

   beards nearly kissing
the ice, feathers distinguishing
   what is bird and not,

much the way I imagine
   Jeoffry and Zooey or even
my own well-loved cat

   will speculate his way into
dark corners trusting
   his whiskers will know

his reach, what he
    may safely return from—the slim
difference between nearly

through and not. His toes
    cringe at the carpet's edge
before the sea of green

    tile, cracked like old anger,
brittle as shell after twenty years
    of shame, but the turkeys

and beyond them
    mallards and swans. No.
Snow geese, mergansers.

COMPLINE

Even Walt Whitman wanted
to put me into a city
of his own devising: brotherly
love. But I refuse his landscape, no
ferryboat, no trolley car, no high-rise
by him yet unseen. Instead give me
a field, this field, dazzled by light,
a dayfield. The blessing of sun
and air revealing green
in deep, empty glister.

Here the lover comes, even
as the light fades, to watch
it go, to watch the goose,
the sparrow, the owl, the slipform
lake, its shore a string. Every
feathered thing, beaded
and bereaved into an endless
Whitmanian line. Patiently
allowing the night, the tender
growing night.

Let no lover be found, not in
the city, not two men
hidden in its dirty scrawl
of noise, in concrete's unbearable
narrowing—but let us be
received into this field. Two men
grasping hands, hands pressed
in prayer to wind, to darkness.
Two men pressed against the grass,
given to giving ourselves to one another.

PLUNDER: HISTORY

Moon of Green Grass. Moon of Hatchings.
Somewhere between here & then—

terra incognita, endless series of vistas,
of horizons, of claims to the land.

Let us name this place after
its original possessors or near

enough, but their name translates
to snake, read as copperhead—

too deadly. Let us honor the terrain
we have crossed & in crossing

have gathered to us, made seamlessly
our own. Land of hides & bone,

of gold & earth yet to be plundered,
of council groves & fence lines, wind

farms & silos dug into the earth
for missiles & yet we can never say

enough. Still it shines & we grasp for it.

Late Morning, Separation

Walking in the fields, driving
the long roads to nowhere
in particular, all was
distance. We did not belong
as a mountain might,
together to its blue. There was

no going further so we sang
teach us to care then
teach us to move on. How
the mountain can unslip its centuries
of hue. But now, who will remember

I held a newborn goat, all damp
heat and legs? Who will I hold
it up to? The finegrain light
through the mist, off the bay
touches the darkpined islands—

The ones newcomers are always mistaking,
                              at first, for mountains.

RIVERS AND MOUNTAINS AT THE END

If I believed in heaven, it would be
        some low-slung valley with scattered
pines & strands of gold-gone aspen.
    Some patches quaking in wind, some not

& sometimes on the same tree
        & since I am dictating belief
I fill my creed with a cloudlessness
    so blue it's mistaken for a movie set

for some old picture, when picture meant
        film & because I can't get enough—
the valley rills with blue, go ahead
    & choose lake or pond or meandering

oxbow. I pronounce this dogma:
        we believe in one valley free
of smoke, no wildfire or flame, no burnt
    offerings, also no development.

Let old heaven & its many mansions all
        recess into ruin, even the great old
gate. Let it fall into earth, become
    artifact of the previous age. But even this—

one person's uncertain paradise too
        is a failure, limited & I am aware
           & yet, it's still mine—
                a kingdom yet to come.

Under the Lawrence Tree, 1929/2021

Look at all that
        sky, blue & black by turn,
the stars hot & certain
           On a copy of a carpenter's bench
              I join you in all that taking-in:
the branches contorting, the depth, the sway
   bird call
            bird call
                    bird call

To lie here as so many
        have, now all the artists turned
to ash, scattered & the tree
        continues beyond all
& will continue to outlast
        the hundred lives who have come
                    under this shade
My eyes unfocus
        & my ears go & they go
home to the ocean, wind
        in boughs across the mountain,
           distant breakers rolling
        1500 miles from the man I've loved
all these years
        as well as I could
Here, take what is offered
        & go, susurrus of wind, magpies
        & their slow rattle, the unending blue
a door, scent of needle duff

We are not meant to stay
            on this mountain; for a moment
I almost lie beside you,
            your dry, sure hand
                        conjured next to mine
Fly buzz
            woodpecker knocking
                        its hellos
wind again against my face
            This might be the closest
we will ever come
            to knowing one another
                        What a life, Georgia,
to go on
            in pigment & imagination.
Eye pondering upwards, body reclined
& rising
            & rising
into those twisted limbs

Sometimes the Truth: Reprise

Wind can plunder
                    a field
as easily as
                    the grass
or light
             which knows
the hours of itself

How a tree
                longs
across generations—
appears a god to
                      the beetle
but as nothing
                    to the stone

If a river can be
a way or a wondering
then let us
                love it
completely
                & momentarily
as the snow when
touching the dark
current, enters it—
                        vanishes

NOTES

The "Plunder" series of poems examine the word plunder from several different viewpoints, using the events and circumstances of 19th century Western US history.

In "Welcome to the Hi-Line," the Hi-Line is the northern region of Montana adjacent to US Highway-2, below the Canadian border. It runs east of the Rockies to the North Dakota border. The epigraph comes from Larry Levis' poem, "Edward Hopper, Hotel Room, 1931."

The narrative in "Beautiful Country" is fictional. It conflates an imagined region of the Blackfoot nation with the factual narrative of Captain Meriwether Lewis killing two Piegans (Blackfeet) in 1806 during the Corps of Discovery Expedition.

The poem, "On Josh Kilpatrick Who Drowned" is after Bruce Snider's poem, 'On Billy Lucas, Who Hanged Himself in His Grandmother's Barn."

"Friday Night, Bannack" refers to the mining boom town of Bannack, named after the region's Bannock Indians. It was Montana's first territorial capital in 1864. Often, due to the shortage of women on the frontier, dances were held where men danced together in both roles.

"Longhair" was a nickname of General George Custer. The poem also riffs on the line "Many a thing are made of pride unaccountable" from Linda Gregg's poem "Unaccountable."

The poem "Winter's Game" takes its inspiration and "winter's room" from Corrie Williamson's poem, "The Valley of a Thousand Haystacks, near Garrison, Montana."

"If Walt Whitman Can Be in a Berkley Supermarket, Allen Ginsberg Can Be in Montana in 1851" is modeled after and pays homage to Allen Ginsberg's poem "A Supermarket in California."

"Slowly Now the Shadows Lengthen" borrows some text from the 1852 hymn "Now the Shadows Slowly Lengthen."

"Convergence// //Conversion" combines several historical and literary sources. The left-hand column recounts the vision of the Salish prophet and holy man Shining Shirt. The right-hand column recounts the four separate delegations made by the Bitterroot Salish tribe to St. Louis, attempting to secure a Jesuit missionary. The accuracy in the telling of the vision of Shining Shirt is not definitive, as it was recorded by white historians and not the Salish people themselves.

In "Reading the Book of Isaiah While Wildfires Burn" the words, "lifted to blue rudiment," comes from "Susurrus Stanzas" by Brian Teare.

In "Beginning with a line by Mildred Walker" the lines, "and you've gone on all these years hating each other" comes from her 1944 novel *Winter Wheat*.

"Cape Disappointment" takes its name from a headland on the northern side of the Columbia River as it enters the Pacific Ocean. This spot was named by John Meares, a British fur trader, in 1788 after he mistook the mouth of a river to be a bay, too shallow for his ship to enter. It is also one of the foggiest places in North America.

In "sxwxwetcheli // hummingbird," *sxwxwetcheli* is the word for hummingbird in the language of the Lummi Nation, a Coast Salish tribe living in Northwest Washington.

"Spring, Bitterroot Valley 1848," makes reference to the first domesticated sheep kept in what would become Montana Territory, by Fr. Pierre-Jean De Smet.

"Compline" borrows the line "the tender growing night" from Walt Whitman.

"Turkeys in Snow" references Edward Hirsch's poem "Wild Gratitude" in which he mentions his cat Zooey. Hirsch's poem is in homage to poet Christopher Smart's poem "Jubilat Agno" or Rejoice in the Lamb, in which Smart mentions his own cat Jeoffry. Both cats are mentioned by name in my poem.

In "Plunder, History," the lines "Let us name this place after / its original possessors or near // enough, but their name translates / to snake, read as copperhead—" refers to the naming of Montana Territory in 1864. One proposed name was Shoshone, to honor the Shoshone Tribe, but legislators pointed out that Shoshone translates to snake. Republicans were worried that Shoshone (snake) might be read as sympathetic to the Confederacy during the Civil War. One of the Confederacy's symbols and names was Copperhead.

"Late Morning, Separation" riffs on T.S. Elliot's line, "teach us to care and not to care" from his poem "Ash Wednesday." The poem also pays homage to the line, "smiling, holding up the new lamb; / whom will he hold it up to?" from Linda Gregg's poem "The Chorus Speaks Her Words as She Dances."

"Under the Lawrence Tree, 1929/2021" references the 1929 painting by Georgia O'Keeffe of a ponderosa pine at night. She painted this tree several times on a summer visit to D.H. Lawrence's ranch outside of Taos, New Mexico. The property is currently owned by the University of New Mexico and the tree still stands.

Acknowledgments

Many thanks to the editors and journals where some of these poems first appeared, sometimes in different versions:

&Change: "If Walt Whitman Can be in a California Supermarket"
Anti-Heroin Chic: "Late Morning, Separation"
Bracken: "Under the Lawrence Tree 1929/2021"
Big Muddy: "Beginning with a line by Mildred Walker"
Court Green: "Field"
diode: "in time the snow is gone"
Empty House Press: "Sometimes the Truth: Reprise"
The Fourth River: "Compline"
Grama Poetry: "anthem"
Invisible City: "Plunder: residential school"
Interim: Plunder: "The Company," "Friday Night, Bannack," "What distance did I know?," "Rivers and Mountains at the End," and "Slowly Now the Shadows Lengthen"
Jubilat: "Now let's talk about resurrection."
Kestrel: "Plunder: Revolver"
The Lake (UK): "[When god wasn't god]"
LandLocked: "On Josh Kilpatrick Who Drowned," and "...to the river"
The Maine Review: "Tilework Illustration of Fox Among Grapevines"
The Meadow: "Beautiful Country"
Montana Public Radio: "A River Is"
Moss: "Reading the Book of Isaiah While Wildfires Burn"
Palette Poetry: "Dramaturgy"
Psaltery & Lyre: "Spring, Bitterroot Valley 1848"
Rust + Moth: "Plunder: History"
San Pedro River Review: "Correspondence"
Sundog Lit: "Welcome to the Hi-Line"
Sweet: A Literary Confection: "In April"
Territory: "Into the Wilderness"
Typehouse Literary Magazine: "Wyeth: Heaven"
Vagabond City Lit: "Sister Self"
Whale Road Review: "Winter's Game"
The White Review (UK): "Turkeys in Snow"

The eight poems whose title begins with the word "Plunder" appeared as a mini digital chapbook for *Ghost City Press'* 2023 Summer Chapbook Series.

Jory Mickelson's first book, *Wilderness//Kingdom*, was winner of a 2020 High Plains Book Award. Their third book, *Picturing* (End of the Line Press), is forthcoming in Canada. Other publications include *Court Green, Poetry Northwest, DIAGRAM, Jubilat, Terrain. org*, and *The Rumpus*. They are the recipient fellowships from the Lambda Literary Foundation, The Desert Rat Writers Residency, Dear Butte, and the Helene Wurlitzer Foundation of New Mexico. They live and write in the Pacific Northwest.

www.ingramcontent.com/pod-product-compliance
Lightning Source LLC
Chambersburg PA
CBHW031440120626
46545CB00006B/2496